The Legend of Marguerite

The Legend of Marguerite

by

GEORGE MARTIN

Introduction, Notes and Editing by D.W.S. Ryan

Jesperson Publishing Limited
St. John's

Jesperson Publishing Limited
39 James Lane
St. John's, NF Canada
A1E 3H3

Cover and Book Design: Donna Snelgrove
Printing and Binding: Jesperson Press Limited
Cover picture: Ish Humber

The publisher acknowledges a financial contribution from the *Cultural Affairs Division* of the *Department of Culture, Recreation and Youth* of the Government of Newfoundland and Labrador which has helped make this publication possible.

Appreciation is also expressed to the *Canada Council* for its assistance in publishing this work.

Printed in Canada.

Canadian Cataloguing in Publication Data

Martin, George, 1822-1900

      The legend of Marguerite

      Includes bibliographical references
      ISBN 0-921692-66-8

1. Roberval, Marguerite de -- Poetry.   I. Ryan, D. W. S. (Donald Wilson Stanley), 1921-   II. Title.

PS8476.A78L44 1995   C811'.4   C95-950251-3
PR9199.2.M37L44 1995

D.W.S. Ryan

CONTENTS

Acknowledgements

Photographs are by Jim and Sharon Ransom, formerly of Harrington, and are used with their kind permission.

Quotes in the Introduction by Elizabeth Boyer are used with her kind permission.

My thanks also to Sharon Ransom for zeroing me in on the Harrington Island locale of the Marguerite legend.

Thanks to Norma Jean Richards of the Newfoundland Legislative Library and to Linda Hodd of the Canadian Literature Research Service, National Library, Ottawa, for providing information about George Martin and his publisher.

D.W.S. Ryan

THE MARGUERITE LEGEND

(a new evaluation — D.W.S. Ryan)

The Marguerite legend is a story of tragic romance. A young girl of noble birth from France, named Marguerite, was a member of a colonizing expedition to the New World. An old nurse who brought up Marguerite accompanied her on the voyage. The expedition set out from La Rochelle, France, in the spring of 1542, destined for New France. Another member of the same expedition, a young soldier, probably also of noble birth, was in love with Marguerite. Unfortunately history has not recorded his name. Both were seeking adventure in the newly discovered world of the West.

The girl's uncle, or close relative, was the leader of the expedition. He was Jean-Francois de la Roque, Sieur de Roberval, a close friend of Francis I, King of France (1494-1547). Francis I appointed Roberval Viceroy of Canada and Newfoundland. This meant Roberval was the sole authority for France in the New World. Roberval, however, was not a sailor. He was a landowner and had spent no time at sea. The chief navigator for the expedition was Jean Alphonse whose writings about the expedition were chiefly concerned with navigational routes. One who did write about the expedition and who recorded Marguerite's tragic story was André Thevet, a Catholic monk who interviewed Marguerite when she returned to France

The expedition, consisting of three ships, left France on the 16 of April, 1542. The first stopping place on this side of the Atlantic was St. John's where they arrived on June 8 and took on fresh supplies of water, wood, salt cod, and fresh salmon. It was the end of July before Roberval left for his destination—Jacques Cartier's colony at Charlesbourg Royal, near what is now named Quebec City. Cartier had left France the previous year, 1541, and started his colony. Roberval was to have joined him that same year, but had difficulty getting his expedition under way. Now a year later he didn't seem to be in a hurry to join Cartier.

While he was resting his crew and replenishing his larder in St. John's, Cartier arrived from Charlesbourg Royal, enroute to France. Cartier's attempt at forming a colony in New France had failed, chiefly because of the hostility of the Indians. The two had a meeting and Roberval urged Cartier, or perhaps ordered him, to return with him up the St. Lawrence, but Cartier would have none of it. Cartier was well aware that it was too late to begin a colony that year, because the growing season was too far advanced, and any hope of surviving the Canadian winter depended on an adequate supply of food. Besides, his colonists had endured enough. Cartier ignored Roberval's orders and slipped out of St. John's under cover of darkness and fog, and headed for France.

Now, three people on the ship that Roberval commanded seemingly hampered his voyage. The first among them was his relative, a young girl called Marguerite, who was an orphan and under his guardianship. Marguerite was in love with a young soldier whom she had known from her girlhood days. It was their show of love for one another that angered Roberval, so much so that he decided to get rid of her along the way. The place he chose was one of the Isles of Demons, the Isle of St. Martha, so named by Cartier in 1535 and renamed "L'iles de la Damoiselle" by Jean Alphonse just after the marooning. It is today one of the Harrington group of islands on the Quebec North Shore and is now called Hospital Island because Sir Wilfred Grenfell set up a hospital there in the early 1900s. In Cartier's time it was believed the islands were possessed by demons. And demons plagued Marguerite during her stay on the island.

Along with Marguerite, Roberval also marooned her old nurse, Damienne, because she had befriended Marguerite during the voyage and tried to hide Marguerite's lovemaking from the eyes of Roberval. Arriving at the Isle of Demons, he had the two put ashore in a boat with a supply of food and all the belongings they'd brought with them for setting up a new home in Canada, including such implements as axe and saw, and four arquebuses.

Marguerite's lover, fearing he might be marooned elsewhere on another island, decided to join them by leaping from the ship, as one version of the legend has it; but recent research by Elizabeth Boyer, an

American writer, states that he was put ashore in a boat, because he, too, took with him his belongings, several bushels of biscuits, canvas, tools, a musical instrument, an arquebus and other things—too much to swim ashore with.

The first thing they did was to survey their surroundings. The island was tree-clad, the soil scanty, and at the base of a rocky hill that overlooked the island was an opening that resembled a cave. It provided them temporary shelter while they were building a cabin of logs. The rock opening is called Margaret's Cave by the residents of Harrington today.

They built a logette without windows, and this sheltered them from the storms, and protected them from roving animals like wolves and polar bears.

Marguerite was the only one who survived the ordeal. She was rescued after spending two years and five months on the island. Her lover survived only eight months there, and the old nurse died early in the winter of the second year, sixteen or seventeen months after they had arrived on the island. A child was born to Marguerite shortly after its father died and lived for seven or eight months, dying just after the old nurse, though in the poem that follows, she dies just before the old nurse. Marguerite's child was the first French child born in Canada.

The Marguerite legend is one of great womanly fortitude and bravery, of great physical stamina and unimaginable endurance. History barely records it, and it has faded from Canadian literature. One who made it the subject of a long poem is relatively forgotten and his book that contains the poem is difficult to locate. He is George Martin, and his book is entitled **Poems**, though on its title page it has the title— **Marguerite; or, the Isle of Demons and Other Poems.** It was published in 1887.

Martin was born in 1822 in County Derry, Ireland, and died in Montreal in 1900. In the light of recent research by Elizabeth Boyer into the Marguerite legend, it is time that George Martin's poem was brought to light again.

In the preface of his book, **Poems,** Martin states that his poems "have been inspired by the history and scenery of Canada, and in collecting them, the author hopes to put in permanent literary form, some of the natural and social aspects which are peculiar to this country." Peculiar indeed is the Marguerite story, an amazing tale of intense human drama associated with stark wilderness survival in the earliest of colonial times.

My first acquaintance with the Marguerite legend was the book, **Ten Canadian Legends**, by Jack Tremblay. It filled a single page, and Belle Isle at the northern tip of Newfoundland was the setting. The graphic sketch that accompanied the thumbnail story fired my imagination. When in 1989 I assembled a small volume of **Legends of Newfoundland and Labrador**, I decided to include the Marguerite legend. At that time I did a fair bit of research but there was very little I could find. Apart from a portion of Thevet's account, I turned up little else. Since **Legends** has been published however, I have discovered a great deal about Marguerite's story, perhaps all there is to know. And it happened this way.

Sharon Ransom of Harrington on Quebec's North Shore came to my house one day to pick up a Grenfell item I had for her. She had read my **Legends of Newfoundland and Labrador**. In the course of our conversation she said to me, "How are you so sure that the Marguerite legend is connected with Belle Isle?" I replied that it was what my limited research indicated.

"Well," said Sharon, "we, from Harrington, think it's Hospital Island, one of the Harrington group of islands, because on Hospital Island there is a cave called Margaret's Cave, and folks there speak of Marguerite whenever the cave is mentioned."

That rekindled my imagination still more.

As a result of that meeting with Sharon Ransom I have learned that the Marguerite legend is very much alive in Harrington, that a writer was there this past summer (1994) doing research for a story on Marguerite, and that an American writer had done extensive research into the legend about two decades ago. She is Elizabeth Boyer, a lawyer, researcher, and novelist. It was through Sharon that I became acquainted with Elizabeth Boyer's documentary research on Marguerite de la Roque. Her work is entitled **A Colony of One: The History of a Brave Woman**. She also wrote a documentary novel—**Marguerite de la Roque, A Story of Survival**. This novel was published in 1975, and her documentary research in 1983. Elizabeth Boyer has put the Marguerite story on the historical plane to which it belongs. Marguerite is an important Canadian historical figure, but the books are still not in our libraries.

In his poem George Martin departs from historical fact in some ways. He gives Marguerite's lover a name, Eugene, which Boyer does not. He also identifies the sex of the child, which Boyer does not. He has Eugene survive the first winter and he has the old nurse die when the baby dies. And he has Marguerite contemplating suicide before the onset

D.W.S. Ryan

of a third winter on the island alone, but is saved from doing so when the sail of a fishing boat heaves in sight, and she is rescued. He also states the relationship of Marguerite to Roberval as niece and uncle, but Boyer states only a close relationship.

Slow at first getting into the story, the poem soon grips the imagination and stirs the emotions with an intense admiration for a young woman who, as Elizabeth Boyer affirms, was "the lone European settler on the northern part of this continent during the winter of 1544."

This poem highlights an important episode in North American history, in particular the history of early settlement in Canada. Of the three that were marooned on the Isle of Demons, Harrington Island, one survived two winters, and a young woman at that. She was, as Elizabeth Boyer points out, "the first European soul to survive more than one winter on American soil, north of Florida and Mexico."

Historians rewriting the early history of Canada should take note of the painstaking research done by Elizabeth Boyer on the Roberval expedition of 1542. It is because of this convincing research that I am compelled to bring to light a literary account of the Marguerite episode of that expedition, a poem that has been forgotten,

I wish also to point out that this introduction to the Marguerite legend corrects errors in my earlier sketch as published in **Legends of Newfoundland and Labrador**.

Readers will note after they have read the poem that it does not conform to historical fact as brought to light recently by Elizabeth Boyer. The poem treats the legend as literature. Elizabeth Boyer's research treats the legend as historical fact. In writing this introduction I have endeavoured to be true to Elizabeth Boyer's factual research as she indisputably presents it in her book, **A Colony of One: The History of A Brave Woman**. The poem should be read as literature. Boyer should be read for the history behind the legend.

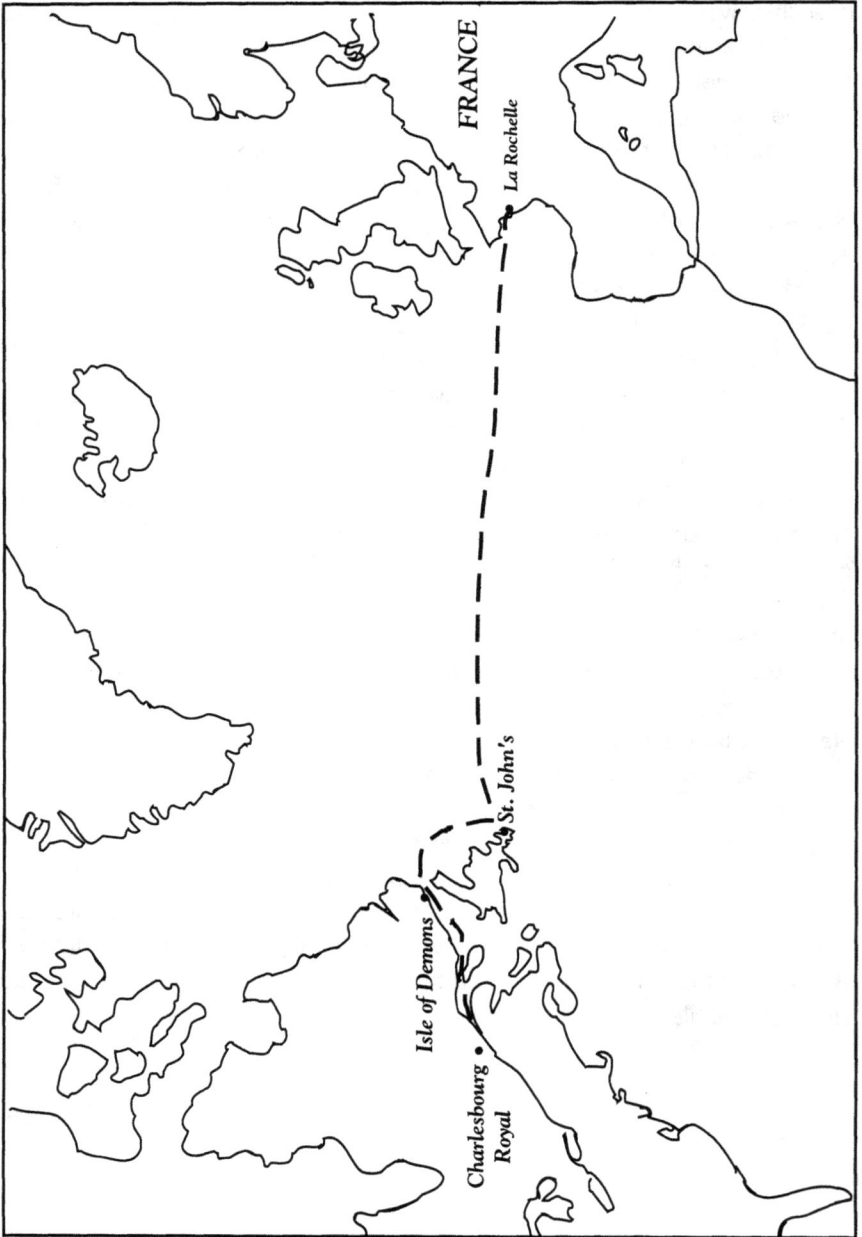

Map showing Roberval's route from La Rochelle, France,1542,
to St. John's to Isle of Demons to Charlesbourg Royal.

D.W.S. Ryan

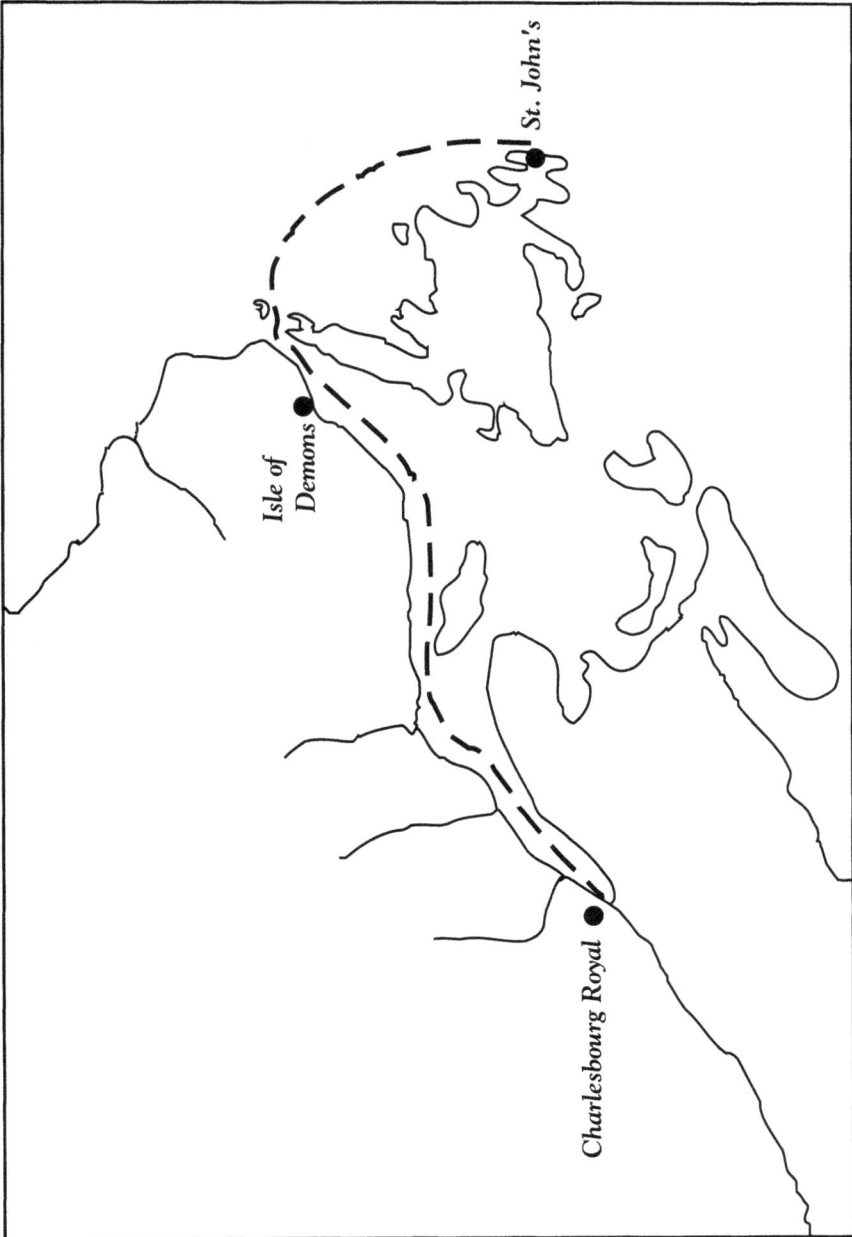

Roberval's route from St. John's to Charlesbourg Royal and
the Isle of Demons where Marguerite was marooned.

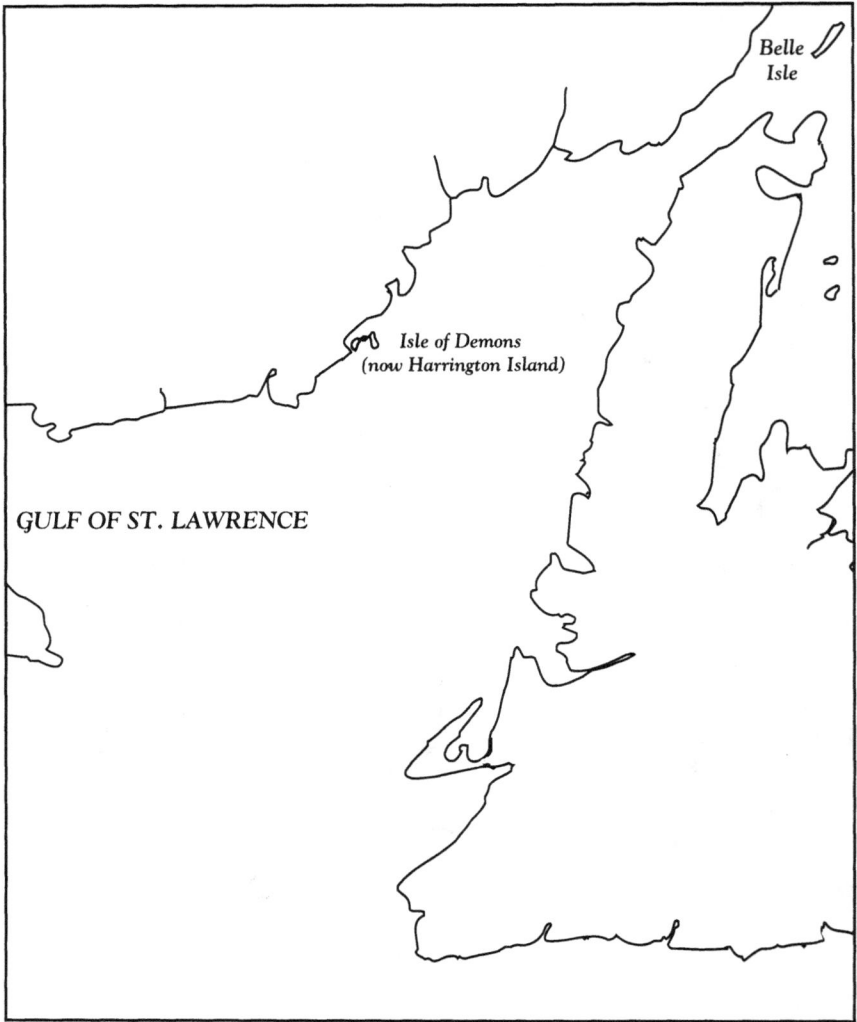

Belle
Isle

Isle of Demons
(now Harrington Island)

GULF OF ST. LAWRENCE

Map showing location of Isle of Demons, now Harrington Island.

D.W.S. Ryan

*Aerial view of the Isle of Demons, now the Harrington Islands,
where Marguerite was marooned*

View of Harrington today, taken from Marguerite's cave.

View of the upper and lower caves—the caves are connected by a crawl passageway inside.

One entrance, upper section—the cave extends inwards about 15 feet.

D.W.S. Ryan

Looking into Marguerite's Cave, upper section. The cave is 4-5 feet high and extends inwards about 15 feet. The flat rock to right is about 5 feet square.

The lower section of Marguerite's Cave—a passageway connects the two. The cave has a southern exposure.

MARGUERITE;

OR, THE ISLE OF DEMONS

AND OTHER POEMS

BY

GEORGE MARTIN.

MONTREAL:
DAWSON BROTHERS, PUBLISHERS.
1887.

Replica of original

MARGUERITE.

PREFATORY NOTE.

The story narrated in the following poem is one of the most touching of the many romantic legends of the early history of Canada. Some foundation in fact it undoubtedly has, for it forms the basis of one of the stories in the collection of Queen Margaret of Navarre, written while the chief actors in the tragedy were alive. The version of Queen Margaret differs from that of Thevet in many respects. He gives for his authorities Roberval and the unfortunate Marguerite herself.

Parkman, in the first volume of his admirable series of histories—the **Pioneers of New France**—gives the story as related by Thevet. The subject readily lends itself to poetical treatment, and, if the heroine in the poem is made to put a more favourable construction upon her conduct than the chronicler, it is surely no more than, as the narrator of her own story, she might have a right to do. The harsh and tyrannical character of Roberval is drawn in dark lines by Parkman. His cruelties, in the short lived colony Cap Rouge, were such that even the Indians were moved to pity for his victims. On his return to France he was assassinated at night in the streets of Paris, probably by the hand of one who had suffered from his tyranny.

In these prosaic days of ocean steamers, cable telegraphs and light-houses, it is difficult to realize the mystery which, in old days, enshrouded the shores of the Western continent. The imaginations of the daring sailors who in their little vessels explored the stormy seas of the West, teemed with stories of dangers, spiritual as well as physical. In those days of supernaturalism, Satan might well stand guard over the great world, where, until then, he had held undivided sway. This Isle of Demons was one of his outposts. On Wytfliet's Map (1597), **I. de las Demonios** is laid down to the North of Newfoundland, but too far out of Roberval's course to be the island of our story. It is necessary to the narrative that the island in question should be in the regular route of vessels, and, as the earliest course of sailors to the Gulf of St. Lawrence was by the Strait of Belle Isle, some of the islands which shelter the harbours of Labrador would probably have been the scene of the events narrated. Jean Alphonse of Saintonge, who was Roberval's first pilot, no doubt indicates the island of our heroine's trials under the name of **Isles de la Demoiselle** in latitude 50°45, and he says there is a good harbour there. This name clung for a long time to the locality and is found on many old maps. To-day the most important of the group is known as Grand Meccatina Island.

SONNET

O Love! thou art the soul's fixed star, whose light—
   A rapture felt through all the rolling years,—
   Absorbs with silent touch the mourner's tears,
A guide, a glory through our mortal night;—
All other passions, be they dark or bright,
   All high desires are but thy subject spheres,
   And captive servitors, whose pathway veers,
Obedient to thine all-pervading might;—
And therefore I no hesitation make
   In choosing thee, a theme accounted old,
Yet ever young, and for poor Marguerite's sake
I trust some kind remembrance to awake
   That shall in tenderest clasp her story hold,
   Even as a rose a drop of dew doth fold.

D.W.S. Ryan

MARGUERITE

OR THE ISLE OF DEMONS

The interior of a Convent in France: Group of Nuns
listening to Marguerite narrating her adventure.

1545.

PART I.

You ask me, Sisters, to relate
The story of the wanton fate
That over sea, with dole and strife
And love and hate enthralled my life,
Entwined with his, whose gentle eyes,
    That never lost their winsome smile,
Illumed for me those sullen skies
    Which canopy the haunted Isle*,
A tale so wild, I pray you think,
    May ill beseem and prove amiss

*the Isle of
Demons, now one
of the Harrington
Islands, in Gulf of
St. Lawrence

For such a hollowed place as this;
A chain it is whose every link
Is rusted with some earthly stain,
The which you may esteem profane
And from its hapless wearer shrink,
I would not, Heaven knows, offend
The sanctity of sinless ears,
    Nor vex the pious soul that hears
Good angels on soft wings descend,
    Illumined, from the starry spheres,
To tread these cloistered aisles and bend
O'er dreaming couches lily pure.
But since your sufferance makes secure,
And since you kindly deign assent,
    And graciously with eager look
    Dispel the fluttering fears that shook
My contrite heart, I am content.

Ave Maria*.

*a prayer on the
rosary to Mary,
the Mother
of God

Mystic Mother! who erewhile
Sought me on the Demons' Isle,
Sought, and with compassion mild
Shielded thy afflicted child;
Shielded, and with vengeance new
Scattered the Satanic crew:
Blest Madonna! aid me now,
Lift the pressure from my brow;
Bid the thunder-cloud depart
From my overladen heart;
Tune my tongue, my lips inspire,
Touch them with celestial fire;
Shape the lay as meet to set,
Like a modest violet,

*virgin martyr of
the early Catholic
Church

In Saint Cecilia's* coronet.

D.W.S. Ryan

Three gallant ships that owned command
Of Roberval's* imperial hand
Thundered to France a proud farewell
And sailed away from brusque Rochelle;
Sailed on a breezy April day,
Sailed westward for a land that lay,
I heard the people wisely tell,
Betwixt the ocean and Cathay.*
From shore to ship, from ship to shore
    A thousand parting signals flew;
    Ah! hopeful hearts, they little knew
That many were there who never more
Must see those faces that faded away,
And were lost in the distance cold and gray.
With troubled breast and tearful eye,
In fear and doubt, I knew not why—
    Unheedful of the sea-winds chill—
    I watched the land recede until
    The mountain peaks had passed from sight,
    Like clouds absorbed in morning's light,
    And ocean's border touched the sky.

*French Viceroy of Canada and Newfoundland who sailed from La Rochelle, France, in 1542 to found a colony in New France.

*Ancient China

Long backward, over leagues of foam,
    My greyhound gazed, —poor **Fida** knew
That he was borne afar from home,
    But not from friends, albeit few,
His still, for better days or worse,
His mistress and her Norman* nurse.
    Far, out beyond the shining bay,
The sister vessels held their way,
Where, gifted with superior speed,
The "Royal Griffin"* takes the lead,
As if she felt and understood
The stern old Viceroy's hasty mood.
    A man of courteous mien was he,

*Normandy was a district of France.

*flagship of the expedition, commanded by Roberval

The Legend of Marguerite

And smooth as any summer sea
When winds are laid; he could be so
When naught befell to rouse the flow
Of passions that with scanty rest
Lay lava-like within his breast.
But Heaven fend or man or woman
    Who set that fiery flood in motion;—
    His anger, like a storm-tossed ocean,
Was fearful in its rage; no human
Expostulation, no appeal
Of speech, or tears, could make him feel
The benediction that is felt
    By one whose soul, if prone to error,
Will yield at last and kindly melt,
    And lay aside its robe of terror.
He could be calm, could well repress
His evil nature's fierce excess,
But only when upon him fell
    The shadow of superior power,
    Then like all tyrants he would cower
And play the courtier passing well.
But no superior save the king
    Had he in all the land of France;
    In Picardy*, his single glance
Was law, religion, everything.

*a province in
northern France

His vassals prized his slightest nod,
And feared him more than fiend or God.
The modest maid, the peasant's bride
His foul approaches must not chide;
I blush, as if it were a sin,
To own him all too near of kin.
Seven sunny years had barely flown
    When I, an only child, was left,
    Of sire and happy home bereft,

D.W.S. Ryan

To wipe a mother's tears alone.
A leader in the wars with Spain,
The hero whom we wept was slain,
Oh! I remember well his look,
    His stature tall and noble brow,
Remember how he often strook*   *stroke
    And praised my long dark hair, and how
On that last morn of clouded bliss
He woke me with a parting kiss;
His hurried prayer, his slow farewell,
    The window flowers, the little room,
    The dangling sword, the nodding plume,
The long top-boots and shining spurs;—
O, let this pass! O, let me quell
    A memory shot through years of gloom.
My comely mother from the hour
    That chronicled his honoured death
Wilted and drooped, a pale sweet flower,
And three years gone I saw her breath
Grow faint and fail. Dear sainted mother!
    'Twas just before her spirit fled
She did beseech her lordly brother*   *Roberval, who
    To shield her orphaned Marguerite's head.   became
He promised with a ready grace   Marguerite's
    And in his rude capricious way   guardian
Thenceforth assigned me fitting place;—
    But I was volatile and gay,
Ready of wit, of skilful hands,
    And minded not his curt commands.

Thus came to pass that on his ship,—
A ringdove in a falcon's grip,—
I sailed the surging seas afar.
But one was there, Eugene Lamar,*   *Marguerite's lover

My bliss, my bane—I cared not what,
Who worshipped me, beside me sat,
And with me paced the giddy deck,
What time we watched the sea-mews peck
The foam that fringed the crested wave.
For me he ventured all, and gave
His fortune to the winds; then why
Should aught disturb, or cause one sigh
To prophesy of lurking harm?

Exultant in their new-found charm,
A motley throng of either sex,
    Of divers rank and variant age
Now promenade the oaken decks,
    Proud of an ocean pilgrimage.
We heeded not their boisterous glee,
    Their merry songs and dancing feet,
    Our happiness was too complete.
The azure sky and emerald sea,
    And free-born winds their magic wrought,
    Till every feeling, every thought,
Involved in tremulous ecstacy
    Made no account of sight or sound;—
    We twain another world had found,
Whose warm excess of drowsing bliss
Excluded all the chills of this.

Our ship sped on, fresh blew the wind,
Her plodding mates lagged far behind;
Like two white cloudlets waxing dim
They hung on the horizon's rim

For many days, but hull and mast
All wholly disappeared at last.

Mid-ocean crossed, the wind blew strong
And like a Nereid's* dolorous song
Wailed through the rigging; rose and fell
The billows with portentous swell.
Swift night came down, cold, wild and black,
Red lightnings lit the inky rack
Of hostile clouds; a storm it grew,
And such a storm as men might rue.
The prince of air his bondage broke,
And loud in horrent thunder spoke;
Our staunch craft felt the perilous strain,
And like a thing in mortal pain
Groaned audibly; strong sails, though furled,
  Were rent in shreds
  From their ash spar beds
And wafted to some calmer world.

*one of the daughters of Poseidon, Greek God of the Sea

Two seamen from the yards were blown;
 An instant mid the tempest's roar,
Above the rattling thunder's tone,
 A double shriek was heard—no more ! —
Their names, their fate, no stone records,
For them no consecrated words,
 Nor bell, nor candle;—only this,
"Two mortals, to the world unknown
 Were blown in the salt abyss."
All night the elements beset
 Our hapless bark; the mad waves leaped

The Legend of Marguerite

Like krakens* on the deck, and reaped

*sea-serpents

A harvest which they garner yet.
Fierce down the hatchways snarled the sea,
   I heard the shout of Roberval
Command them closed; ah me! ah me!
   What prayers! what shrieks! I never shall,
   While memory marks the flight of years,
Forget that storm of phrenzied* fears.

*frenzied

Think not our sex alone gave way
   To craven doubt and blanched despair;—
Great burly men, whose heads were gray,
   Gave wildest wings to desperate prayer.
I dare believe they felt ashamed,—
The blessed Saints whose names were named
In phrase that seemed impiety.

What marvel if at such a time
   My lover groped his way to where
   My couch was spread, and tarried there?
Was such devotedness a crime?
Together on the floor we knelt
In quiet hopefulness, and felt

*Jesus of
Galilee

Assurance in our souls that He*,
Who walked the waves of Galilee,
When, weak of faith and sore afraid,

*see
Matthew 8:23-27

The sinking Peter* cried for aid,
Would manifest His sacred will;
   Would stretch His saving hand and bind
   The fury of the maddened wind,
And bid the savage waves be still.
My greyhound, ever near me, took
A painful and bewildered look;
All that dread night the narrow space
He traversed with unwearied pace.
The imminent danger well he knew,

32

D.W.S. Ryan

And watched the changes of my face,
    And moaned at its unwonted hue.

The morn broke fair but other storm,
    More dreadful that the wrath of heaven,
Or rage of hell, began to form;
    The high-bred gossips, envy-driven
Did look askance, and whisper blame,
And young Lamar's and Marguerite's name
Were caught at, with but slight excuse,
As playthings for their wanton use.
Soon drifting round my uncle's ears
The idle tale in wrath he hears,
And starting from his proud repose
His fury like a whirlwind rose
And suddenly upon us burst.
I heard my name most foully curst
And coupled with a word of shame;
My tear-drenched cheeks grew all aflame;
Beside me, where I trembling stood,
    My watchful **Fida** whined and growled;
    The glaring maniac on him scowled,
His eyes two throbbing balls of blood,
And choking with some fiery word,
Drew forth and waved his gleaming sword,
Then smote the faithful brute;—his neck
Received the edge; athwart the deck
The severed head the slayer spurned:
    O God! I saw a sea of gore,
From which my eyes in horror turned;—
    I swooned and recked of nothing more,
When from that death-like sleep I woke
    Lamar's moist eyes were near my face,
Some tender words he softly spoke,—
    My languid arms his neck embrace,

My lips their wonted banquet share,
And breathe again the vital air.
Ah! never since that hour when whirled
Around with me a crimson world
Have I forgot or ceased to mourn
    The playmate of my childhood's years;
    (Pardon, I pray, these silly tears.)
His long slim neck had often borne
My cheek, when tired with romping play
Under a chestnut's shade we lay,
His taper head flexed backward, till
His loving eyes had gazed their fill.

Harsh prelude this! a warning fit
Of coming woes. The brow hard-knit,
The curling lip and heaving chest
Of Roberval presaged the rest.
But what his dark design might be
Eluded anxious scrutiny;
We only knew some purpose dire,
Like a swollen adder cirqued with fire,
Lay coiled within his vengeful heart,
Ready against our lives to dart.
    "Fear not, my love!" Eugene exclaimed,
    "Faint not, true heart! whose peace is spilt;
The evil tongues that have defamed
    Thy innocence shall own their guilt.
If blame there be 'tis I alone
    Have erred, nor do I shrink to bear
Thy kinsman's wrath, but how atone
    For wrong committed unaware?
Let unjust Roberval decree
    What punishment his ire may crave;
However tends his evil course,
He cannot, dearest one, divorce

My constant soul from thine—from thee,
    For even from the silent grave
I verily believe my love
Would issue through the cope above,
And mingling with the volant air
Pursue thy beauty alway, where
On any spot of land or sea
My Marguerite might chance to be."
His voice failed—tremulous, his eyes
Such passion held as well might save
A world from wreck; our wedded sighs
Made interlude to honied speech,
And bound us closer, each to each.

On flew the ship; a bounteous gale
Fed to repletion every sail,
And Tethys*, turbulent no more,
    Advanced her banners, green and white,

*Greek goddess
of the sea

    (In sooth it was a goodly sight)
Toward the wild Hesperian* shore.
At length glad signs of land were seen,

*the shores of the
New World

    Strange birds, a friendly escort, came
    And perched upon the spars, so tame,
So numbed and wearied with the keen
Cold journey it had been no feat
To clasp their wings; but who could treat
Those little rovers of the sea,
That claimed our hospitality,
With less than Christian charity?
Westward across the ridgy waste
My uncle gazed as if in haste
To reach the promised port, but no!—
    His thought to other ends was set,
As soon the traitor meant to show,
With sudden stride, his hot brow wet

In oozing wrath, he gave command:
"Steer north-by-west!" The wonderland
Of Norumbega* hove in sight,

And outlined in a purple light
The dreaded **Isle of Demons** lay;
Thither the **Griffin** bore away.
I saw the treacherous villain smile,
  And as the ship was drawing near
The marge of that unholy Isle
  I saw the sailors quake with fear.
A boat was launched, provisioned, stored
With arms and ammunition, oared
And quickly manned;—for what? for where
Let my false guardian's tongue declare.
"Go! wretched girl," he fiercely said,
  As, from the ship, myself and nurse
  He hurried, "Go, and take my curse,
All evil light upon thy head!"

Hence to the **Demons' Isle,** a place
  Than which, save hell, there is no worse,
And ponder o'er thy rank disgrace;
There only foul-faced devils dwell,
As every seaman here can tell.
Hence! and prefer thy dainty charms
To glad some princely demon's arms.
Dishonour on my house, my name,
Confusion, everlasting shame,
Thou and thy paramour have wrought;
For him, I swear he shall be taught

What torture means;—the crippled crone*
Who all your secret sins has known
And pandered to, let her partake
  The punishment assigned to you,

D.W.S. Ryan

A penance to such service due.
And when your threads of life shall break,
Then may you both for ages ache,
    Conjoined in purgatorial fires,
    Sure antidote to lewd desires."
His insults pierced like barbs of steel;
    My patience I no longer nursed,
    I bade the tyrant do his worst:—
O, if he thought to see me kneel,
And for his mercy humbly sue,
'Twas little of his niece he knew;
His curse, his terrors, I defied,
And told him in his teeth, he lied!*
I even dared predict his fate; (1)
"Foredoomed," I said, "to all men's hate,
Like Cain* or Judas* thou shalt die
Unhoused, where none will pause to sigh
Denied the pity you deny."
He winced and wondered, powerless
    To check such unexpected scorn.
    A strength miraculous, new born
In uncontrollable excess,
From God or fiend I questioned not,
Through all my rigid being shot.
The boat received and swiftly bore
Its convicts to the fearful shore.
There all my fortitude departed,
And lorn and lost and broken-hearted
I stood upon the windy beach,
And stretched my hands as if to reach
The idol of my widowed soul.
"Farewell! dear friend Eugene, farewell!
Those breakers that between us roll
    Shall sound for me a fitting knell
When thou art borne I know not where."
Thus did my sorrow load the air.
He saw, he seemed to hear my wail,
And springing from the forward rail
Leapt in the sea, and bravely smote

(1) See note at the
end of the poem.

*Cain who killed
Abel and was
banished to
be a wanderer

*Judas who
betrayed
Jesus and who
hanged himself

The Legend of Marguerite

With lusty arms the foamy flood,
Oh! how my hot impetuous blood
Surged through my veins; while still remote
He battled shoreward gallantly;
Now borne upon a toppling wave,
And blinded by the surfy spray,
Now lost to sight, now seen again,
While on the ship some fearless men
Loud shouts of exultation gave;
Then others into tumult broke,
Whose cheers the Island echoes woke.
But Roberval, whose stormy face
Flamed like a furnace, fiendish, base,
With levelled arquebuse took aim
Straight at the swimmer, shrieks of "Shame!"
He heeded not; the bullets sped,
And whistled past my hero's head.
A few more strokes and he is safe!
The jagged rocks his strong limbs chafe,
But soon the slippery sands are gained
And I am to his bosom strained.
Their coifs the women, wild with gladness,
Stripped from their heads and, in their madness,
Flung to the waves, an offering fair
In witness of the Virgin's care,
My solace in the gulphs of sadness.
From stem to stern the furor ruled,
And Roberval chagrined, befooled,
His sails reset, and sailed away,
But half avenged; and we were left
Of all the peopled world bereft,
To hell's dark brood a helpless prey.
But for that he I loved was still
Linked to my fate, for good or ill,
My thanks to gracious Heaven I wept.
The poor old nurse behind us crept,
And kneeling on the salty ground,
A benediction even there,
In answer to her silent prayer,
Deep in her withered heart she found.

D.W.S. Ryan

The ship was gone, and with it went
    All hope of ever seeing more
    The glory of our native shore;
I knew our cruel banishment
Was purposed for a lingering death,
A dirige* of painful breath.   *dirge
Was it in mercy he bestowed
The food and arms, a goodly load?
Nay, these were meant to stretch the doom
That made the Isle an open tomb.
"Mourn not—sweetheart!" Eugene began,
"Here where the sea-winds rudely fan
Thy queenly brow, a queen to me
Henceforward thou shalt truly be;
And if thou choose to reign alone
    I'll be thy faithful paladin*,   *knight
    And many a noble trophy win
In honour of thy virgin throne.
Then come, while yet the lord of day
    Dispenses light and gentle heat,
And let us hand and hand survey
    The wonders of our new retreat.
    This little kingdom, Marguerite!
Encircled by the shining sea,
Is large enough for thee and me."
'Twas thus in cheerful mood he sought
To lure the current of my thought
From cypress shades to run abroad
In pleasant ways, approved of God;
Nor sought in vain: my spirit caught
The hue, the blessedness, the glow
That love's endearing words bestow,
And like a lark that sudden springs
From barren lands and soaring sings,
Rose heavenward on hopeful wings.

But hark! the vesper **angelus***
In holy accents, tremulous,
Now calls us to the Virgin's shrine.
If still your wishes fair incline
To follow this capricious clue
 To-morrow after open dawn
 I'll join you on the eastern lawn,
Under the lindens, and pursue
My story to its tragic close.

PART II

The tale continued in the Convent grounds; the same group of Nuns listening.

How softly have my limbs reposed!
 Nor stormy sea, nor haunted land,
 Nor sorcerer's unhallowed wand,
Disturbed the opiate shades that closed
 The sleepy avenues of sense;
 And therefore I, without pretence
Of weariness or dream-wrought gloom,
My tale of yester-eve resume.

*Isle of
Demons
where they
were marooned
Together o'er the mystic Isle*
We wandered many a sinuous mile.

D.W.S. Ryan

'Twas midway in the month of June,
And rivulets with lisping rune,
And bowering trees of tender green,
And flowering shrubs their trunks between
Enticed our steps till gloaming gray
Upon the pathless forest lay.
Think not I journeyed void of fear;
 Sir Roberval's hot malediction
Like hurling thunder sounded near;
Our steps the envious demons haunted,
 And peeped, or seemed to peep and leer,
 From rocky clefts and caverns drear.
But still defiantly, undaunted,
Eugene averred it had been held
By wise philosophers of eld
That all such sights and sounds are mere
Fantastic tricks of eye and ear,
 And only meet for tales of fiction.
"Heed not," he said, "the vicious threat,
 'Twas but a ruffian's empty talk,
The which I pray thou may'st forget
 And half his evil purpose baulk."
A silent doubt and grateful kiss
Was all I could oppose to this.
But firmer grew my steps. The air
 Was laden with delicious balm;
Rich exhalations everywhere,
 From pine and spruce and cedar grove,
And over all a dreamy calm,
 An affluence of brooding love,
A palpable, beneficent
Sufficiency of blest content.

Amid the hours, in restful pause
 We loitered on the moss-clad rocks,

And listened to the sober caws
　　Of lonely rooks, and watched thick flocks
Of pigeons passing overhead;
Or where the scarlet grosbeak sped,
　　A wingéd fire, through clumps of pine
Sent chasing looks of joy and wonder.
　　Blue violets and celandine,
And modest ferns that glanced from under
Gray-hooded boulders, seemed to say—
"O, tarry, gentle folk; O, stay,
　　For we are lonely in this wood,
And sigh for human sympathy
　　To cheer our days of solitude."
Meek forest flowers, how dear to me!
　　I loved them, kissed them on the stem,
And felt that I must ever be
　　Secluded from the world like them.

The long-drawn shadows, eastward cast,
Admonished us that day was fast
Dissolving, and would soon be past;
And we must needs regain the spot
　　Where waited good Nanette* our coming.

*her old nurse

The chattering squirrel we heeded not,
　　Nor paused to list the partridge drumming.
The wedded bird was in her nest,
　　And knew from the suspended song
(A tribute to her listening ear)
That from the green boughs rustling near
　　Had trilled and warbled all day long,
A brief space only must she wait
The fondling of her chirping mate.
With some wise meaning, wise and deep
That from her eyes was fain to peep,

D.W.S. Ryan

And wealth of words and lifted hands
    Our thoughtful servitor, Nanette,
    Gave kindly greeting ere we met.
"Come, children, follow me," she said,
And silently the way she led
    An arpent* from the ocean sands,
Directly to a piny grove,
Where she with wondrous skill had wove
A double bower of evergreen,
Meet for a fairy king and queen.—
"There, tell your rosaries and take
A sabbath slumber; till you wake,
Nanette, hard by, will watchful stand,
With loaded arquebuse in hand,
Your trusty sentinel, for here
Some prowling beast may chance appear
On no good neighbour's lawful quest;
To-morrow I can doze and rest."—
Thus, voluble, my faithful Nurse.
    Amazed, I stood and could not speak,
    But kissed her on the brow and cheek,
And wept to think my Uncle's curse*
Should fall on her, so worn and bent,
So moved with every good intent.

*a short stroll

*the wrath of
Roberval

A flushing joy it was to see
    That double-chambered arbour fair,
Re-calling to my memory
    The storied lore of things that were
My childhood's moonlit witchery.
Next morn we sought the circling strand
    And question made of wind and sea
    If such a thing might ever be,
That, soon or late, from any land
Some friendly sail would come that way

And waft us thence: in vain, in vain!
The hollow wind had nought to say,
But, like a troubled ghost, passed by;—
The waste illimitable main
And awful silence of the sky
Vouchsafed no sign, made no reply.—
Oft times upon some lifted rock
That overhung the waves, we sate
And listened to the undershock
Whose sad persistency, like fate,
Made land and sea more desolate.

Again in lighter mood we trod
The yellow sands and pale-green sod
Strewn with innumerable shells,
In whose pink whorls and breathing cells
Beauty and wonder slept enshrined,
Like holy thoughts in a dreamer's mind.
Of these sea-waifs an ample store
We gathered, and at twilight bore
The treasure to our sylvan home*.

*forest home

Once more the star encumbered dome
Of heaven its thrilling story told,
And Dian*, lovely as of old,

*Diana,
Roman
goddess of
the moon

Poured lavishly her pallid sheen
Upon that tranquil world of green;
Whose cool and dewy depths, now rife
With luminous and noiseless life,
Responded wide; the fire-fly race
In myriads lit their tiny lamps;
As an army's countless camps
The warder in some woody place
At nightfall on his watch may trace;
So gleamed and flashed those mimic lamps.

D.W.S. Ryan

The third day came. From shore to shore,
Adventurous ever more and more,
Our penal Isle we wandered o'er.—
Which way our roving fancy led,
A wilding beauty largely spread
Rewarded our ambitious feet,
And made our banishment too sweet
For further censure or repining.
　　Now culling flowers of dainty dyes,
　　Now chasing gaudy butterflies,
And now on herbaged slopes reclining,
Where purple blooms of lilac trees,
And sultry hum of hermit bees
Disarmed the hours of weariness.—
Nor can you fail, dear friends, to guess
　　That time for dalliance* we found,—
And if we loved to an excess
In many a long involved caress,
　　O think how we were cribbed and bound.—
Lush nature and necessity,
　　As witnessed by the Saints above,
　　In one delicious circle wove
The pulsings of our destiny.

*love making

The great rude world was far away,
And like a troubled vision lay
Outside our thought; its cold deceits,
The babble of its noisy streets,
And all the selfish rivalry
That courts and castles propagate
Were alien to our new estate.—
A fragment of propitious sky,
Whereon a puff of cloud might lie,
Through verdured boughs o'er-arching seen,
And glimpses of the sea between

The Legend of Marguerite

Far stretches of majestic trees,
Such peaceful sanctities as these
Were our abiding joyance now.

Cheerily and with lifted brow
Eugene led on, where tamaracks grew,
And where tall elms their shadows threw
Athwart a little glen wherein
A virgin brook seemed glad to win
The pressure of our thirsty lips.
        Pleasant it was to linger there
And cool our fevered finger-tips
        In that pellucid stream and share
The solace of the ocean breeze.
        For summer heats were now aglow,
The fox sat down and took his ease,
        The hare moved purposeless and slow;
But louder rang the blue jay's scream,
        The woodpecker tapped the naked tree,
        Nor ceased the simple chickadee
To twitter in the noonday beam.—

My lover, wheresoe'er we strayed,
        Made search in every charmed nook,
        And angled in the winding brook
For all sweet flowers that love the shade
To twine for me a bridal braid.
Pale yellow lilies, nursed by rocks
Rifted and scarred by lightning shocks,

D.W.S. Ryan

Or earthquake; river buds and pinks,
     And modest snow-drops, pearly white,
     And lilies of the vale unite
Their beauty in close-loving links
Around a scented woodbine fair
To coronate my dark brown hair.
The fragile fern and clover sweet
On that enchanted circlet meet;
Young roses lent their blushing hues,
Nor could the cedar leaf refuse
With helmet flowers to intertwine
Its glossy amplitude divine.—
Emerging from that solemn wood,
High on a rocky cliff we stood
At set of sun, far, far away
The splendors of departing day
Upon the barren ocean lay.—

There on that lone sea-beaten height,
Investured in a golden light,
Eugene, with looks half sad, whole sweet,
Upon my brow the garland set,
At once a chaplet and aigrette*,
And said: "Be crowned, my Marguerite!
My own true soul, my ever dear
     Companion in this wilderness.
Though hopeful still, I sometimes fear
     That days of darkness and distress
May come to thee when woods are sere,—
When it may baffle all my skill
To guard thee from white winter's chill;—
But hence all raven-thoughts of ill,
Let me believe that Nature will
Relax her rigour, having caught
     The soft infection of those eyes

*head wreath
adorned with
a feather

In whose blue depths my image lies,
Even as my soul, with love distraught,
Like a lone star drowned in the sea,
Is wholly drowned and lost in thee.—
Love is our own essential being,
    Sole sovereign over utmost fate,
Its own sufficient laws decreeing,
    Immortal and immaculate;
And when this mild ethereal flame
    To mortal man was kindly given
    'Twas surely meant by highest Heaven
That never aught of evil name
Should dare attempt to thwart its power.—
Then let us, dearest, from this hour
Defy the future, and pursue
The unimagined pleasure due
To such surpassing love as ours.
    One moment in thy folding arms
Alone in these sequestered bowers;
One throb of thy impassioned heart,
    Now speaking audibly to mine,
And saying "It were death to part;"
    One honey-dew caress of thine,
    Out-sums a million rude alarms,
Out-lives whole centuries that weigh
On loveless souls, on sordid clay,
That gravitate to ways of shame,
And know love's magic but by name.—
These roseate skies will change their hue;
    This pomp of leaves when autumn lowers
The windy ways of earth will strew;
    This aromatic crown of flowers,
Made sacred now since worn by you,
To-morrow will begin to fade.—
    But love, sweet spirit, linked as ours,
By sad vicissitude o'erlaid,
Endures, unchanged by any breath
    Of adverse fate, and surely will
    Life's last inevitable chill

Survive, and triumph over death."—
     Thus, eloquent, the radiant youth,
Like one inspired with sacred truth,
Fair as Adonis*, o'er me breathed
The incense of pure love, and wreathed
My heart in dewy dreams of bliss.
     Consenting Nature, pleased the while,
     Bestowed upon her outcast Isle
     The magic of a mother's smile.
Spent Sol* impressed his warmest kiss
On ocean's brow; the wanton wind
Went sighing up and down to find
     Meet objects for his soft embrace
All things to amity inclined;
     Fierce bird and beast forebore to chase
Their feeble prey, as if they felt
Love's universal breathings melt
Their savage instincts; everywhere,
Like mute enchantment in the air,
This subtle permeating power
Reigned sole. O, blest ambrosial* hour!
O, halcyon* days that followed after,
With music from my lute, and laughter,
And song and jest, and such full measure
Of secret love's exhaustless treasure
As gave to pain the wings of pleasure!—

So fled our summer dream, as flies
An angel through cerulean* skies
     On some good errand swiftly bent,
So brief its stay that ere we wist,
Gruff Autumn, garmented in mist.
     His courier winds before him sent,
The which, equipped with sleet and hail,
Beat down as with an iron flail

*a Greek youth
famed for his
beauty

*sun

*heavenly

*pleasant,
peaceful

*clear blue

The grandeur of the woods, and left
Their naked solitudes bereft
Of bird and flower. The trees stood stark
And desolate against the dark
Chaotic sky. The mighty sea
    Its billows hurled upon the shore
    As if resolved to over-pour
And gulph our prison-house. Ah, me!
All roofless now, save here and there
    A tall pine stretched its spear-shaped head
Aloft into the gelid* air;
    The hemlock, too, its beauty spread,
A tent-like pyramid of green,
Symbols of hope amid a scene
    Where hope grew pale at winter's tread.

*winter impending

No more, along the sounding shore,
In hushed voluptuous dells, no more,
Nor on the perilous rock which gave
Rude welcome to the climbing wave,
Might we, in amplitude of joy,
Our paradisal hours employ,—
From green to gray, from gray to white,
    So rapidly the change came on,
It seemed but the work of a single night
    And all our faery world was gone.—
Down came the snow, compact, hard-driven
By all the scourging blasts of heaven,
Until, like clouds, dethroned and hurled
Tumultuous to this nether* world,
Around the desert isle it lay,
A rampart to the ocean's spray.

*earthly

D.W.S. Ryan

Half hid where friendly pine trees spread
Perpetual shelter overhead,
Hugging a hillside lifted high
Betwixt us and the arctic sky,
Our cabin stood; a poor defence
Against the mute omnipotence
Of searching and insidious frost,
Which, like a ghoul* condemned and lost,   *preying ghost
The closeness of an inmate claimed;—
But on the rustic hearthstone flamed
Dry wood and pine-knots resinous!
     A ready and abundant hoard
     When days were long our hands had stored
Against the season perilous;
And good Nanette, 'twas her desire
To feed the bickering tongues of fire
That warned the dumb intruder hence.

When night fell thick, I loved to sit
And watch the fire-gleams fall and flit
On wooden walls and birch-bark ceiling,
Among the densest shadows stealing,
Till these, in folds and festoons golden,
Like tapestry of castles olden,
Shifted and fluttered free, revealing
To fancy's charmed and wiser vision
Such fabrics as in looms elysian*   *heavenly
The angels weave; and thus our hut
A palace seemed; and was it not
More beautiful, illumed the while
By dear Eugene's adoring smile,
Than many a royal chamber where,
Concealed amid the gloss and glare,
A thousand hateful evils are?—

The Legend of Marguerite   51

Such fare as woodland wilds afford,
Supplied our ever-cheerful board;
Nor such alone; the salt sea wave
Its tributary largess gave,
All that our lenten wants might crave.

Slow crept the whitened months, so slow—
    I sometimes felt I never more
Should see the pretty roses blow,
Or tread on aught but endless snow,
    And listen to the nightly roar
Of tempest and the ocean flow.
Weird voices, woven with the wind,
Riding on darkness often came
And syllabled the buried name
Of Roberval, which, like a hearse,
Bore inward to my palsied mind
The ghost of his inhuman curse.

Was it sick fancy, sore misled,
That to my shuddering spirit said?—
"Those sounds that shake the midnight air,
Are threats of Shapes that will not spare

territory Your trespass on their fief accurst."
    "Hush, hush, my love," Eugene would say,
"That cry which o'er our cabin burst,
    Came from the owls, perched royally
Among the pine-tops; you but heard
The language of some beast or bird;
The mooing of a mother bear,
An hungered in her frozen lair;
The laugh and mooing of the loon
That welcometh the rising moon.

D.W.S. Ryan

The howling of the wolves you hear,
In chase of some unhappy deer,
Impeded in its desperate flight
     By deep and thickly crusted snows,
     O'er which its lighter-footed foes
Pursue like shadows of the night.
That lengthened groan, that fearful shriek
Was but the grinding stress and creak
Of aged trees; they seem to feel
The wrench of storms, and make appeal
For mercy; in their ducts and cells
The sap, which is their life-blood, swells
When frosts prevail and bursts asunder
With sharp report its prison walls;
Then cease, beloved, to fear and wonder
     For all these harmless peals and calls.
In sweet assurance rest, love, rest
Thy head on this devoted breast,
And dream sweet dreams; the gentle spring
Will come anon, and birds will sing
As sweetly as they sang last year;
And shall I not be ever near
To share with thee the murmuring
Of waking life? the humble bee
Will drone again as blissfully
As when from flower to flower he went
And to the choral symphony
His basso horn serenely lent."—
My fears were laid; I ceased to think;
Athirst and eager still to drink
The nectar of his speech.

                    How oft,
     If he but chanced to hear me sigh
When wild winds blew, or when the soft

And flaky harvest of the sky
Descended silent, he would sit
     Under that snow-thatched roof and tell
Such marvellous tales of mirth and wit,
     They held me like a wizard's spell.
Or else some poet's plaintive verse
     That breathed soft vows of youth and maiden,
     With love-begotten sorrow laden,
In twilight tones he would rehearse;
And whilst the rhythmic measure flowed
     From those attuned lips, my breast
With trepidation heaved and glowed,
     For in such guise was well expressed
The master-passion's undertone,
     Or happy or disconsolate,
     Of many a lover's wayward fate
That bore some semblance to our own.

'Twere over-much to pause and tell
How slid the weeks, and all befell
Ere we could to the heavens say,
     "The terror of your rage is past,
     The gnawing frost, the biting blast,
morning sun   And life is in the matin ray."—
The swallow came, the heron's scream
     Athwart the marsh-lands, through the woods,
Sped resonant; I ceased to dream
     Of demons, and my waking moods
The radiance of the morning took.
Upon the bare brown leaves I stood,
     And saw and heard with raptured look
     The gleam and murmur of the brook,
Which we in summer's plenitude
     Had traced to many an arbored nook.

D.W.S. Ryan

'Twas midmost in the budding May,
    Whilst on my couch of cedar boughs,
Perturbed with nameless fears I lay,
    And breathed to Heaven my silent vows,—
A cloud-like cope of purple hue
    Descended o'er me, hid me quite,
And seemed a soft wind round it blew,
And from the mystic wind a voice
    Spoke low: "Poor child of darkened light!
The pure of heart are Heaven's choice;
The Virgin who hath seen thy tears,
In pity for thy tender years,
Will aid thee in thine utmost plight."
A hallowed tremor o'er me crept,
And in that purple cloud I slept
Enshrined, how long I never knew;—
And through my dreams the soft wind blew
Like music heard at dusk or dawn,
And when I woke and found it gone,
In fullness of great joy I wept.

'Twas thus a new revealment came,
    A something out of nothingness,
To which we gave the simple name
    Of Lua. O, the first caress
A mother to her first-born gives!—
    Methinks the angels must confess,
Through all the after ages' lives,
An influence so pure and holy,
That human hearts, the proud and lowly
Are touched thereby. I kissed, and kissed
My pretty babe, and through the mist
Of happy tears upon it gazed
In silent thankfulness, and praised

The Empress of the skies, whose grace
Had glorified that humble place.

The sandy marge again we trod
Round the green Isle, and felt that God
Was very near,—in ocean's roar,
    And in the zephyr's* scented breath,
In summer green, in winter hoar,
    In joy, in grief, in life, in death,
Our Friend and Father evermore.

*soft west wind

Again across the naked sea,—
    In tumult or in blank repose,
    At morn and noon, and evening close,—
Sick yearnings from our souls were sent.
    But bootless still the hungry sigh,
A southward sail still southward went,
    If any such we might descry,—
As twice or thrice it chanced to be,
We saw or fancied shimmering,
Like a white eagle's outstretched wing,
Hiding the strait and dubious space
That separates the lifted face
    Of ocean from the stooping sky.
The sail would melt, the hollow dome
Above us and our prison home,
And girdling waves, and sobbing rain,
    And winds full-fledged,—all things that were
    Of earth and sky, of sea and air,
    Strangled sweet Hope, and in the pit
    Of outer darkness buried it.

D.W.S. Ryan

Yet seemed it sinful to complain,
When to our feast of love was given
The fairest fruit that gracious Heaven
Had e'er for human joyance shed.
Sweet Innocence! the small hands spread,
Dimpled and white, catching at things
    Viewless to us, but clearly seen
By those wide-open eyes; the wings
    Of heavenly guests it must have been
Fluttering near the sinless child,
Azure and golden, till she smiled
    And shrank from their excessive sheen.

Again the forest's green arcades
Gladly we paced; their sunlit shades
Investured us; the laughing brook
    That solaced us the year before,
Mirrored again my lingering look;
In that clear glass I could not fail
To see my face grown somewhat pale,
    But not less fair; we trod once more
The lofty cliff whereon Eugene
Had crowned me his bride and queen.
Pleasant those summer days to walk
Where no intrusive step could baulk
Our happiness; no tongue to dare
Whisper disparagement, and bare
The mysteries of Love's free-will,
Approved of Heaven to strive for still,
The liberty that angels share.—
Another summer's beauty dead,
    Another winter's cerements* wound   *shrouds, snow
    On tree and shrub; the sheeted ground,
The cruel storm-land overhead,
The scream of frightened birds, the wind
    That in its teeth the tree-tops took
    And worried all day long and shook,
These and the monstrous ocean blind

With foamy wrath, were ours once more;—
    Once more within our cabin mewed
Under the pine tops, crisp and hoar,
    My fears their old alarms pursued.

Four times the moon had waxed and waned
    Since summer blooms, so bright and brief,
    Were mourned for by the falling leaf,
And winter winds were all unchained,
When came the direful, fatal day.
    The Spectre of the wide world came
In league with winter's fierce array,
    In league with fiends that hissed the name
Of Death around the ruined Isle.

Deep lay the snow, pile heaped on pile,
When food fell scant, and on a morn,
Ere yet the infant light was born,
Eager-thus alway to provide,
Eugene forsook my drowsy side,
And lavished on my happy lips
His silent love; then gently slips,
Upon the little callow heap
That lay embalmed in downy sleep
His softest kisses: happy child!
She made a little stir and smiled,
As if in soothest dreams she knew
Whence came that quiet fond adieu.
Then pausing at the windy door,
    His arquebuse on shoulder laid,
    And in his belt a shining blade,

His brow a troubled shadow wore;—
Or was it but my own blurred thought
A semblance of foreboding wrought?
Backward he moved, a tardy pace,
And toward me turned his comely face
And said: "Dear love, I thought to go
Ere thou shouldst wake, for well I know
These frequent partings, though but brief,
Aye touch thy tender heart with grief."
"Loud blows the nor-wind," I replied.

    "Surely thou needst not haste away
    Before the leaden eyes of Day
On our small world are opened wide;
For all these partings, my Eugene,
Are bitter drops that fall between
Our honied draughts of happiness;
    Ah! well I know what dangerous toil,
What weary hours companionless,
    Are thine in quest of needful spoil,
Be-wrenched, from stubborn wood and wave,
Wherein—Oh God!—an early grave
May compass thee; and I remain
    A wretched mourner, doomed to bear
The burning curse and bitter bane
    Bequeathed me by Sir Roberval;—
    O stay, Eugene, stay yet awhile!
Just now I dreamt I saw thee borne
By Shapes unshapely, stark and shorn,
    Three times around the darkened Isle;
Then did the heavens o'er thee bend,
And in a cloud thou didst ascend,
Lost to the world and me forever."
    "'Twas but a dream," he said, "no more,"
But saying which, a painful quiver
    His lips betrayed, then cheerily bore
His manly head, and thus made end.
"No evil can such dreams portend:—
Nor need I, dearest, say farewell;

For love and faith cannot deceive,
And hence I cannot but believe,
What holy whispers round me tell,
That though thou tarriest here behind,
    Thy spirit journeyeth with me,
    Clasping me round whereso I be,
A shelter from the bruising wind,
    A covert from the drenching sea.
Then rest, my own brave Marguerite,
    Rest thee in trust; 'tis meet that I
    The savage elements defy
For thy loved sake, and for the sweet,
Sweet sake of her who slumbers there,
Pillowed upon her golden hair,
Her beauty, love, so like thine own;—
    Sweet babe! dear wife!" Ere I could speak
    He kissed the tear-drop from my cheek,
And ere I wist I was alone,
    The door stood wide, and he had passed
    Into the dusky void, and vast
Uncertainties concealed by Fate.
Ah, me! I could but watch and wait
For his return. For his return?
I felt my heart within me burn,
Then sicken to an icy dread,
For seemed a sad voice near me said,
"Thou ne'er shall see his face again!"

finest example   The paragon of noblest men!
It could not be; I would not own
A prophecy that turned to stone
All joys that I had ever known.

The wind increased, the day wore on,
And ere the hour was half-way gone
That follows noon, a storm of snow

D.W.S. Ryan

Blinded the heavens, and denser grew,
 And fiercer still the fierce wind blew
As night approached, a night of woe,
 Such as no fiend might add thereto.

The double darkness walled us in,
 The blackness of the storm and night,
And still he came not! O, what sin,
 What blasphemy against the light
Of Heaven had my soul committed?
 Never before had eventide
Once found him absent from my side.
Eugene came not! deceived, outwitted,
 Sore tempest-tossed and lured astray,
By demons, when the night-owl flitted
 Across his face at close of day,
Groping for home, exhausted, faint,
No angel near, no pitying saint
 To aid his steps and point the way.

From ebb of day till noon of night,
And onward till return of light,
The signal horn, Nanette and I,
Alternate blew, but for reply
The wind's unprecedented roar,
And ocean thundering round the shore
Our labor mocked; and other sounds,
Nor of the land, nor sea, nor sky,
Our ears profaned; the unleashed hounds
Of spleenful hell were all abroad,
And round our snow-bound cabin trod,
And stormed on clashing wings aloof,
And stamped upon the yielding roof,
And all our lamentation jeered.

Down the wide chimney-gorge they peered
    With great green eye-balls fringed with flame;—
The holy cross I kissed and reared,
    And in sweet Mary's blessed name,
Who erst had buoyed my sinking heart,
Conjured the foul-faced fiends depart.
Their shriekings made a storm more loud
Than that before whose fury bowed
The hundred-ringéd oaken trees;
More fearful, more appalling these
Than thunder from the thunder-cloud;
But trembling at the sacred sign,
And mention of the Name divine,
They dared not, could not disobey,
But fled in baffled rage away.—

The morrow came, and still the morrow,
But neither time, nor pain, nor sorrow,
Nor any evil thing could make
My stricken soul advisement take
Of aught that in the world of sense

*will of God The fiat of Omnipotence *

Might choose prescribe; I only know
That fever came, whose fiery flow
Surged through the temple-gates of thought,
Till merciful delirium wrought
Release from knowledge, from a world
Where Death's black banner stood unfurled.—

Restored—condemned—to conscious life,
The parting hour, the storm, the strife,

D.W.S. Ryan

Rose from their tombs and dimly passed,
But on my spirit only cast
A feeble shade. When known the worst,
When every joy that love has nursed
Lies cold and dead, a sullen calm
Sheds on the bleeding heart a balm
That is not peace, and does not heal,
But makes it half content to feel
    The frost upon the withered leaf,
To see love's lifeboat rock and reel
    And founder on the stormy reef.

A languid stupor, chill and gray,
Upon my listless being lay—
I knew and felt Eugene was not;—
I saw that in the osier cot*,
Constructed by his cunning skill,
My babe lay sleeping, very still:
So very still and pale was she,
That when I questioned, quietly,
How long since she had fallen asleep,
Nanette could only moan and weep,
And rock her body to and fro.—
With cautious step, and stooping low,
I took the little dimpled hand
    In mine, and felt the waxen brow.
    O, Queen of Heaven! clearly now,
'Twas given me to understand
That all the warmth of life had fled;
My babe, my pretty babe, was dead!—
In stupefaction fixed I stood
    Smitten afresh; a wailing cry,
The wounded love of motherhood,
    Rose from my heart; mine eyes were dry
Denied the blessed drops that give
A little ease, that we may live—
Live on, to feel with every breath
That life is but the mask of death.

*cot made of
willow branches

The Legend of Marguerite   63

Regardful of my frozen gaze,
    Hard set upon the frozen face,
Nanette, at length, in halting phrase,
    Her painful pass essayed to trace:
Told how, when hot the fever ran
Along my veins, and when the wan
And wasted moonshine fringed the hearth,
And voices that were not of earth
Came through the gloom, the famished child,
With pouting lips and eyelids mild,
Her wonted nourishment did crave;
And how, O god forgive! she gave
The little mouth its wish. She told
How dismal were the nights and cold,
Her haunted hours of rest how few,
And how my precious darling drew
From the distempered fevered fount
    The malady that raged in me.
How long it was, the tangled count,
    One week or two, or maybe three—
Her head astray, she could not tell,
When rang, she said a silvery bell,
A-tolling softly far away.
    So softly tolling, faint and far,
    When quiet as the morning star,
That cannot brook the glare of day,
And seeks the upper azure deep,
My Lua (pardon if I weep),
Pure nestling of this sinful breast,
Had struggled into gracious rest.

Unhappy nurse! that hallowed knell
Which on her pious fancy fell
Through midnight dreams was solace meet
For one whose slow, uncertain feet

D.W.S. Ryan

Their journey's end had well-nigh gained;
Whose meagre face drooped, pinched and pained,
From ague*-fits that lately shook   *fever
All gladness from its kindly look.
No longer in those furrows played
The gleams of mirth that erst had made
Her gossip by the cabin fire,
A pleasing hum; for she had store
Of gruesome tales and faery lore,
Which suited with the elfin quire
Of winds that on the waste of night.
Their voices spent; 'twas her delight,
In calmer hours, her voice to strain
     With lays of roving Troubadour*   *minstrels,
That from her girlhood's bloom had lain   singers of love
     Mid memory's tuneful cords secure.   songs and folk
How changed she was! soon, soon I felt   tales
My pity for her dolour melt.
My friend and sole companion now,—
I brushed the gray hairs from her brow
And kissed it; then came back to me
The days when on that palsied knee
I perched, a happy child; where late
My babe, my second self had sate:—
Strange orbiting of time and fate.
Hid in the upheaved scarp of rock
That screened our hut from winter's shock
A cave there was of spacious bound,
Wherein no wave of human sound
Had ever rolled; imprisoned there,
Like a grey penitent at prayer,
Hoar Silence wept, and from the tears
     Embroidered hangings, fold on fold,
     And silver tassels tinct with gold
The fingering of voiceless years
Had deftly wrought, and on the walls
In sumptuous breadth of foamy falls
The product of their genius hung.
     From floor to ceiling, arched and high—

The Legend of Marguerite   65

A counterfeited cloudy sky,—
Smooth alabaster pillars spring.
On either side might one espy
What seemed hushed oratories * rare

*chapels

Inviting sinful knees to prayer.

Into that chapel-like retreat,
Untrod before by human feet,
The wicker cot, wherein still lay
My Lua's uncorrupted clay
We bore, and in an alcove's shade
Our tear-dewed burthen softly laid.
Long muffled in my heavy woe,
    I knelt beside the little bed
    And many a tearful Ave* said.

*prayer

At length, at length, I rose to go,
But kneeling still, my poor Nanette,
Her crucifix and beads of jet
Clasped in her praying hands, stirred not,
    Nor spoke;—our flickering lamp
    Through the sepulchral gloom and damp
Made sickly twilight round the cot.
Orbed in her upturned hollow eyes
Two tear-drops gleamed. I said, "Arise!
Come, come away. Good sister, come!"
Still motionless as death and dumb,—
I shook her gently, spoke again,
    When sudden horror and affright
Laid hold upon my reeling brain;

*without
having
made
confession

    Her soul, unshrived*, had winged its flight!—
I sank upon the clammy stone,
The lamp died out and all was night.
"Mother of God! alone! alone!"
    I cried in agonized despair,
    "O pity me! O Mary spare!

D.W.S. Ryan

A mother's anguish hast thou known,
O pity me! alone! alone!"
A thousand startled echoes sprang
Forth from their stony crypts, and rang
A ghostly miserere round
The cavern's dread Cimmerian* bound,
Till sinking to a dying moan
They answered back, "alone! alone!"

*mythical people
who lived in
perpetual
darkness

"Nay, not alone, poor Marguerite!"
I heard a voice divinely sweet,
And in a moment's awful space
That silent subterranean place
Was filled with light;—I did not dream:
In beauty and in love supreme,
Before me shone our Lady's face
(O would I could behold it now)
The coronal upon her brow,
With star-like jewels thickly set,
    The Sovereign presence certified.
Pure as the snow that lingered yet
    On solemn heights, with sunrise dyed,
Her raiment gleamed. "Weep not," she said,
    And toward me stretched her sacred hands
As if to raise my drooping head;
    "Be comforted! the triple bands
        Of grief and pain
Which Death around thy heart has coiled
        Shall part in twain;
If secret sin thy soul hath soiled,
If thou thy lover loved too well,
The Seraphs* say in high debate,
'Better excessive love than hate,
        Save hate of hell.'
If fiends infest this desert Isle

*the highest
of the
nine orders
of angels

Regard them not; the soul whose trust
On Heaven leans, may calmly smile
At Satan's utmost stretch of guile
    And tread down evil things like dust.
The working of the wicked curse
Branded upon thyself and nurse
Shall cease with dawn of hallowed days;
    She fitting sepulture hath found
    Under and yet not under ground;
    Here leave her kneeling by the child,
Here, where the power thy God displays
    Shall keep their bodies undefiled,
Shall change to marble, flesh and bone.
Then come , and leave the dead alone;
Come hence!—thy round of days complete,
Thy babe and lover shalt thou meet
      In Paradise.
      Look up, arise!
My hands will guide thy fainting feet."
She led me to the outer light,
    And ere a second breath I drew,
    Ere I could fix my dazzled view,
She vanished from my misted sight.

Resigned, uplifted, forth I went,
But, oh! 'tis hard to nurse content
In silent walls; to ever meet
With filling eyes the vacant seat;
To tread from day to day alone
The silent ways, familiar grown,
Where dear companionship has shed
A glory and a rapture fled;
Where every hillock, tree and stone
Are memories of a loved one, dead!

                    D.W.S. Ryan

Again the flowering springtime came,
    The wedding-time of happy birds,
But not, oh! not for me the same;
    To whom could I address fond words?
The violet and maple leaf,
Had they but known my wintry grief,
They would not have appeared so soon.
    I could not bear to look upon
    The beauty of the kindling dawn,
Nor sunset, nor the rising moon,
    Nor listen to the wooing notes
    That warbled from a thousand throats,
From cool of morn till heat of noon.
My soul was with the wind that sighed
Among the tree-tops; all the wide
Waste desolation of the sea
Possessed me; I could not agree
With aught of earth or firmament.
Where could I go? which way I went
His melancholy shade did glide
Behind the rocks, among the trees,
And whispered in the twilight breeze
Endearments whispered long ago.
    In constancy of love and fear
    My sick heart bore his heavy bier,
How lovingly the angels know.

I knew not of my lost love's tomb,
Whether amid the shrouding gloom
Of some tenebrous yawning chasm,
Or in the watery world's abysm,
He met those spectres of my dream;
No trace, no sign, no faintest gleam
Did all my questing ever show.
'Twas well, perchance, that this was so;

The Legend of Marguerite

But may I not believe that yet,
Long after we again have met,
I shall know all? shall hear him tell
What on that dreadful night befell,
And how when in the toils of death
He called me with his latest breath
And blessed me? It will magnify
The joys of that dear home on high
If memory keep our bygone woe,
Our grievings of this world below.

A huntress of the woods I grew,
　　Necessity my frailty taught
To track the fleetest quarry through
The forest, wet with morning dew,
　　Unheedful of the bruises wrought
On tender feet; the wounds received
From thorns whose leafy garb deceived
My glowing limbs. My loosened hair
　　I freely gave to every wind,
　　Content to feel it stream behind,
Or drift across my bosom bare.

So passed the uneventful days,
The sad monotony of weeks,
Till August suns had ceased to blaze;
　　Till o'er the forest's hectic cheeks
A languishing and slumbering haze,
　　The mellow Indian Summer crept;
　　It was as if chaste Dryads* wept
At sign of Winter's coming tread,

*mythical
nymphs of the
woods and trees

　　　　　　　　　　　　　　　　　D.W.S. Ryan

Till from their falling tears was spread
Those exhalations o'er the woods
Amid whose greenest solitudes
    Their festivals of joy they kept.

So came the Autumn's ruddy prime,
    And all my hopes, which had no morrow,
Like sea-weed cast upon the beach,
Like drift-wood barely out of reach
    Of waves that were attuned to sorrow,
Lay lifeless on the strand of time.

So ebbed my life till beamed the hour
When burst in sudden bloom the flower
Of merciful deliverance.
That day I walked as in a trance,
My dismal round, as was my wont,
To many a joy forsaken haunt
Where oft upon my lover's breast
My head had lain in blissful rest,
Till coming to that sea-beat height
Where erst, enrobed in golden light,
His hands, aglow with love conferred
    Upon my brow the spousal* wreath,
    Whilst heaven and all things underneath
His words of sweet adorement heard.
There failed my limbs, and long I sate
At one with thoughts grown desperate.
Two winters had I known since first
I stood upon that Isle accurst,
The third a near, and how could I

*Her marriage was a common-law one in which two persons in the presence of a witness—in her case the old nurse—married each other without the benefit of clergy.

Its killing frosts and snows defy?
Surely 'twere better now to die.
So ran my thoughts, and fair in sight
The breakers tossed their plumes of white,
The same as on that fearful day
When bravely through their blinding spray
My menaced lover fought his way.
I listened to their luring speech
Till lost in lornest fantasy;
Till toward me they did seem to reach
White jewelled hands to join with mine.
I rose and answered: "I am thine,
Thou desolate and widowed Sea,
That late hath come to pity me.
My lost Eugene! 'neath yonder wave
    Oh should thy faithful Marguerite
    Thy lonely corse in darkness meet
How calm, how blest will be my grave !
Sweet babe, adieu! and thou, Nanette
With tearful eyes on Heaven set,
Thy watch beside my Lua keep."
Forward I stepped, prepared to leap;—
One loving thought, one hasty glance
Sent o'er the deep to sunny France,
When hove directly into view
A sail, a ship! could it be true?
Or but a phantom sent to mock
My madness on that lonely rock?
Agape I stood with staring eyes
An instant, then my frantic cries
Went o'er the deep, they heard, they saw,
Those mariners, and from the maw
Of Death my timely rescue made.
    My Country's flag the good ship bore,
And just as day began to fade
    We parted from that fatal shore,
And long ere moonrise many a mile
To northward loomed the Demon's Isle.
Soon homeward bound, again I trod

D.W.S. Ryan

My native soil, and thanked my God
For that on me he deigned to smile.

Here ends my tale. And now, I pray,
If I have stumbled on the way,
Have shown but little tuneful skill
In this wild chant of good and ill,
My faults, my frowardness forgive.
Here, a sad vestal*, let me live,   *virgin priestess
And share with you the peaceful bliss
That points a better world than this;
Here shall I seek from Heaven to win
Forgiveness for my days of sin;
Here shall my soul in prayer ascend
For him I loved; my godlike friend,
My Husband! if that honored name
Is due to one who naught of blame,
No falsehood, no unmanly art
Ere harbored in his open heart,
Then truly can nor ban nor bar
Deny it to the lost Lamar.
And if at times his spirit flits,
    Even here within this holy place,
    With mournful eyes before my face,
And by my couch in silence sits
Till blooms the morn, I dare not pray
The gently shade to haste away.

(1) NOTE TO P. 24.— The settlement of Roberval at Quebec was a disastrous failure. It is said that the King, in great need of Roberval, sent Cartier to bring him home. It is said, too, that, in after years, the Viceroy essayed to repossess himself of his transatlantic domain, and lost his life in the attempt. Thevet, on the other hand, with ample means of learning the truth, affirms that Roberval was slain at night, near the Church of the Innocents, in the heart of Paris.— Parkman, Pioneers of France. (This footnote was appended by George Martin.)

The Legend of Marguerite

ABOUT THE POET

George Martin is not a well-known Canadian poet. Little is written of him and his poetry is difficult to find. He is barely mentioned in the Macmillan **"Dictionary of Canadian Biography"** and his poetry is not at all familiar. I have not found him mentioned in any poetry anthology, and his only volume of poetry is not easy to come by. Our libraries do not have a copy and no copy was available in the National Library at Ottawa when I made an enquiry a few years ago. My copy came through a secondhand book dealer. I went in search of his poetry when I came across a few lines from his poem, "Marguerite", mentioned in connection with the Marguerite legend that I was researching a few years ago.

We know the following about George Martin:

* He was born in Ireland in 1822 and came to Canada when he was ten years old;

* He attended Black River Literary Institute at Watertown, New York;

* He later settled in Montreal and studied photography;

* He was a friend to English-born poet, Charles Heavysege (1816-1876), who was six years older than Martin and who had already published a volume of poetry before he came to Canada.

When Martin came to Canada it was a new country, not yet having attained nationhood. He was in his mid-forties when the Fathers of

Confederation met at Charlottetown in 1867 and drafted the British North America Act which brought Ontario, Quebec, New Brunswick, and Nova Scotia into union. There were strong stirrings in the air about nationhood, and one of its advocating and exuberant voices was a young Irishman, Thomas D'Arcy McGee (1825-1868). Speaking in the Legislative Assembly in Quebec on May 2, 1860, McGee said:

"I look to the future of my adopted country with hope, though not without anxiety; I see in the not remote distance one great nationality bound, like the shield of Achilles, by the blue rim of Ocean....I see a generation of industrious, contented, moral men, free in name and in fact—men capable of maintaining, in peace and in war, a Constitution worthy of such a country."

McGee was a journalist, poet, lecturer, and politician and was an influential figure among the young literary Montrealers. Martin had contact with McGee, being a fellow Irishman, and they were members of a literary club in Montreal. Ballad writing was a poetic form that they engaged in to varying degrees. McGee published **"Canadian Ballads and Occasional Verses"** in 1858. It was almost thirty years later that Martin published his **"Poems"**, containing the long narrative "Marguerite". In his volume of poetry he pays tribute to Thomas D'Arcy McGee and Charles Heavysege. His tribute to McGee was written on the day that McGee was assassinated. McGee was a man of the people, an outstanding public figure. Of McGee, Martin wrote:

"The Poet and Statesman lies cold in his gore,
His eloquent accents will thrill us no more:
No more, with our hearts to all charities strung,
Shall we listen to catch the sweet sounds of his tongue.
That tongue, whose enchantment could hold us in thrall
Will never more gladden the close, crowded hall;
But the light of his genius will shine o'er the land,
And his fame, like Mount Royal, forever shall stand,
For his thoughts were the lights of our northern sky,
And his soul's spoken melody never can die...."

Martin wrote of his friend, Charles Heavysege, a very private person:
"So child-like, modest, reticent,
With head in meditation bent
He walked our streets!...."

D.W.S. Ryan

Martin was a man of Heavysege's kind more so than of McGee's. He was, states D.J. O'Donoghue in **The Poets of Ireland**, "at one time considered to be one of the leading poets of Canada." Whereas he is practically unknown today, Martin made a not-insignificant contribution to Canadian literature and history in his tributes to Thomas D'Arcy McGee and Charles Heavysege but more appealingly in his immortalizing of Marguerite in his long dramatic poem of that title. He seized upon an incident out of Canadian folklore and poetically dramatized it in good style. His "Marguerite" poem is historically revealing but not so historically factual. He has treated the character, Marguerite, with sensitivity and understanding. A young French damoiselle of noble birth, marooned on an island on the Quebec North Shore with her old nurse and lover and surviving almost two and half years, is a tale that is asking to be read today. It is a poem that will give today's young adolescents a glimpse into the earliest of attempts to colonize our land. Readers who want the historically factual account of the Marguerite episode, its place and importance in Canadian history, should read Elizabeth's Boyer's book, **"A Colony of One: The History of a Brave Woman"**. Elizabeth Boyer has also written a documentary novel about Marguerite. This book, too, is very enlightening.

In bringing the poem "Marguerite" to light, I feel I am giving George Martin a literary recognition that has long been neglected. I hope also that I am giving Canadians generally an acquaintance with an episode in our national colonial history that deserves more recognition. The Marguerite legend that now has a place in Canadian literature, thanks to the research of Elizabeth Boyer, now has a surer place in Canadian history.

Sources

re Marguerite:

Boyer, Elizabeth. **A Colony of One. The History of a Brave Woman.** Ohio, Veritie Press, 1983

— **Marguerite de la Roque: A Story of Survival.** Ohio, Veritie Press, 1975.

Thevet, André. **Cosmographie Universelle.** (as included in Elizabeth Boyer's **A Colony of One**)

The address for Veritie Press is P.O. Box 222,
Novelty, Ohio, USA 44072

re George Martin and publisher:

Klinck, Carl F. et al. (editors). **Literary History of Canada. Canadian Literature in English.** Second edition, Vol. I. Toronto & Buffalo, University of Toronto Press, 1976.

O'Donoghue, D.J. **The Poets of Ireland.** London, Henry Frowde, Oxford University Press, 1912.

Parker, George L. **The Beginnings of the Book Trade in Canada.** Toronto, University of Toronto Press, 1985.

Wallace, W. Stewart. **The Macmillan Dictionary of Canadian Biography.** Toronto, Macmillan, 1963,

www.ingramcontent.com/pod-product-compliance
Lightning Source LLC
Chambersburg PA
CBHW050602280326
41933CB00011B/1950